I LOOK LIKE THIS

(Draw a picture of yourself here)

THIS BOOK BELONGS TO . . . .

I LIVE IN . . . .

I AM . . . . YEARS OLD

MY FAVOURITE PLACE IS . . . .

MY DREAM IS TO . . . .

. . . .

"We shall dream of the ever increasing gales,
the birds in their Northward flight;

The magic of twilight colours,
the gloom of the long, long night ...

Though the grip of the frost may be cruel,
and relentless its icy hold,

Yet it knit our hearts together in that
darkness stern and cold."

–Ernest Shackleton

Shackleton's Journey Activity Book is © Flying Eye Books 2015.
All artwork and text within are © William Grill 2015.

Written and edited by Zelda Turner.

Published by Flying Eye Books, an imprint of Nobrow Ltd.
62 Great Eastern Street, London, EC2A 3QR.

Published in the US by Flying Eye Books, an imprint of Nobrow (US) Inc.,
611 Broadway, Suite #742, NY 10012, New York, USA

ISBN 978-1-909263-80-2

Printed in Poland on FSC assured paper.

William Grill

SHACKLETON'S JOURNEY

ACTIVITY BOOK

Written & Edited by Zelda Turner

FLYING EYE BOOKS

LONDON ✽ NEW YORK

A STORY OF UNIMAGINABLE PERIL

ANYONE CAN BE AN EXPLORER.

From a young age, Ernest Shackleton knew this. Born in Ireland on 15 February 1874, the second of ten children, he was always a keen reader and the books he read made him restless for adventure. He left school at 16 to go to sea.

Life as an apprentice sailor was "hard and dirty work," but the young Shackleton was thrilled to travel the world and dreamed of big things ahead. "I felt strangely drawn to the mysterious south," he told reporters. "I vowed to myself that some day I would go on and on 'til I came to one of the poles of the Earth."

 He was almost the first to reach the South Pole – twice! First as an officer on Captain Scott's Discovery expedition; then in 1908, he came within 97 miles of the Pole on his own Nimrod expedition. Three years later, the Norwegian explorer Roald Amundsen beat everyone to it.

SHACKLETON REALISED THAT THERE WAS ONLY ONE GREAT CHALLENGE LEFT – to cross the frozen heart of Antarctica, all the way from one sea to the other. Back in London, he raised funds to support his trip. He bought a ship, named it Endurance, and with the help of his second-in-command, Frank Wild, recruited a crew of 26 men (from the 5,000 who applied), along with 69 sledge dogs to pull supplies and equipment.

ENDURANCE SET SAIL ON 8 AUGUST 1914. The crew's last stop before heading for Antarctica was a remote whaling station on South Georgia Island. Norwegian whalers told Shackleton that it was a bad year for ice. But ever the optimist, he decided to press on.

IN JANUARY 1915, ENDURANCE BECAME TRAPPED in thick pack ice in the Weddell Sea. Stuck, as one crewmate put it, "like an almond in the middle of a chocolate bar." The men tried everything to get her free, but Endurance wouldn't budge. For ten months, loud cracks and deafening sounds were heard as the ice jammed hard against her thick wooden walls. Finally, after what Wild called "the bravest and most gallant fight ever put up by a ship," she was crushed beyond hope of repair, and eventually sank.

Shackleton remained positive in front of the crew. "So now we'll go home," he remarked calmly. A new challenge rested on his shoulders: their mission now was to survive.

STRANDED THOUSANDS OF MILES FROM HOME, with no way to communicate with the outside world, the men camped on the sea ice for six months, eating penguin and burning seal blubber for fuel.

When the ice began to break up, they made a dash for uninhabited Elephant Island in three lifeboats salvaged from the Endurance, dodging ice floes and killer whales circling in the darkness.

After 16 long months, the crew had found solid ground. But their troubles were not over yet. Knowing that rescue would never come to such a desolate spot, Shackleton bravely set out again with five of his men to get help.

THEY SAILED AND ROWED 800 MILES IN A TINY LIFEBOAT, battling the stormiest seas on Earth, before landing on the wrong side of South Georgia Island – then almost died trekking non-stop for 36 hours across ice and snow and unmapped mountains to reach the whaling station in Stromness.

Four months and three failed attempts later, Shackleton returned to Elephant Island on 30 August 1916 to rescue the rest of his men. Astonishingly, all of them were alive!

The story of how Shackleton and his crew managed to survive this epic adventure became legend, a testament to their courage and endurance. Like many great tales, it reminds us that there is a whole world out there to discover and great challenges to overcome.

What young explorer hasn't dreamed of running off to sea? How about serenading penguins with a banjo; fighting ferocious sea leopards; conquering unmapped mountains, or building a den out of a couple of upturned rowing boats?

Your Adventure Starts Here!

This book puts you in Shackleton's shoes, testing your resourcefulness at every turn. And it will have you thinking up your own adventures – the kind other children can only dream about. Open it on any page. Fill the blank spaces with your ideas and artwork, maps and plans for future exploration.

And challenge yourself and your friends to the limit with the ultimate Game of Endurance, at the back!

"Adventure is just bad planning."

– Roald Amundsen,
Norwegian polar explorer

CHOOSE YOUR OWN ADVENTURE

What unexplored part of the world – island, mountain, ocean, desert or even planet – would you like to discover? DRAW A MAP TO EXPLAIN TO OTHERS HOW YOU WILL GET THERE.

CHOOSE YOUR OWN ADVENTURE

WHAT'S YOUR MOTTO?

Shackleton named his ship Endurance after his family motto, "By Endurance We Conquer" – words he lived by in life. Circle the words you like best to find a motto that suits you. Or make up your own from scratch.

ALWAYS ...

Dream

Dare

Smile

Try

Create

Brush your teeth

Have a laugh

Make a difference

Make a mess

Explore

NEVER ...

Give up

Worry

Grow old

Say never

Be late

Stop trying

Fail

Be embarrassed

Go to bed before midnight

Forget

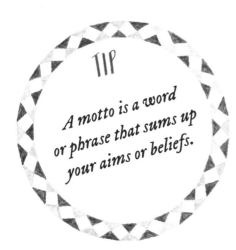

TIP

A motto is a word or phrase that sums up your aims or beliefs.

... Is all you need

Fun	A friend	A smile
Love	Adventure	Sweets
Money	Power	Knowledge
	Faith	

Be ...

Awesome	Happy	Yourself
Prepared	Surprising	Different
Kind	Smart	Curious
	Bold	

My new motto is ....

....

....

....

FACT

The Endurance was one of the strongest
wooden vessels ever built, and designed specifically
for harsh polar conditions. Its bow (the front) was 1.3
metres thick and could be used as a battering ram,
"shattering the floes in grand style," as one
crewmate put it.

DESIGN A SHIP FOR YOUR EXPEDITION

Does it have any special features? What is it called? DRAW YOURSELF AS THE CAPTAIN.

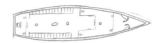

DECIDE WHO YOU WANT ON YOUR CREW

BY CIRCLING THE TEN QUALITIES THAT SUM THEM UP BEST ON THIS PAGE.

Curious

Resourceful

Tidy

Disciplined

Adventurous

Tough

Courageous

Loyal

Optimistic

Entertaining

Ambitious

Generous

Laidback

Stylish

Determined

Playful

Cheerful

Hilarious

Reliable

Easy-going

Intelligent

Unflappable

Quiet

Imaginative

Witty

Famous

FACT

Shackleton handpicked a crew of 26 officers, sailors, scientists and escapists. He quizzed potential sailors on their practical skills, but was also interested in more unusual things, like if they could sing well or make people laugh. He was a good judge of character and personality mattered more than expertise.

Clumsy

Honest

Trustworthy

Motivated

Stubborn

Sensible

Charming

Cool

Good-looking

Impulsive

Ticklish

Moody

Chatty

Eccentric

Thoughtful

Calm

Kind

Practical

Bossy

Lucky

Strong

Polite

Observant

No-nonsense

Diplomatic

FACT

Legend has it that Shackleton's crew responded to his call
for adventure after seeing an ad that read, "Men wanted for
hazardous journey. Small wages. Bitter cold. Long months
of complete darkness. Constant danger. Safe
return doubtful. Honour and recognition
in case of success."

WRITE A SHORT ADVERT

TO RECRUIT VOLUNTEERS FOR YOUR EXPEDITION.

Highlight the nature of your adventure, likely dangers, and what skills you're looking for.

THE CREW

Finish the drawing by adding the features of any friends or family you've decided to recruit.

FACT

The Norwegian flag was the first to be planted at the South Pole, by Roald Amundsen. It was still there when the British Expedition, led by Captain Scott, made it to the spot a month later. "Great God!" wrote Scott, "This is an awful place." Terribly disappointed to come second, and already in bad shape, Scott and his men perished on the long journey back. Their frozen bodies were found, half-buried in snow, months later.

DRAW A FLAG

— REAL OR IMAGINED — TO FLY ON YOUR EXPEDITION.

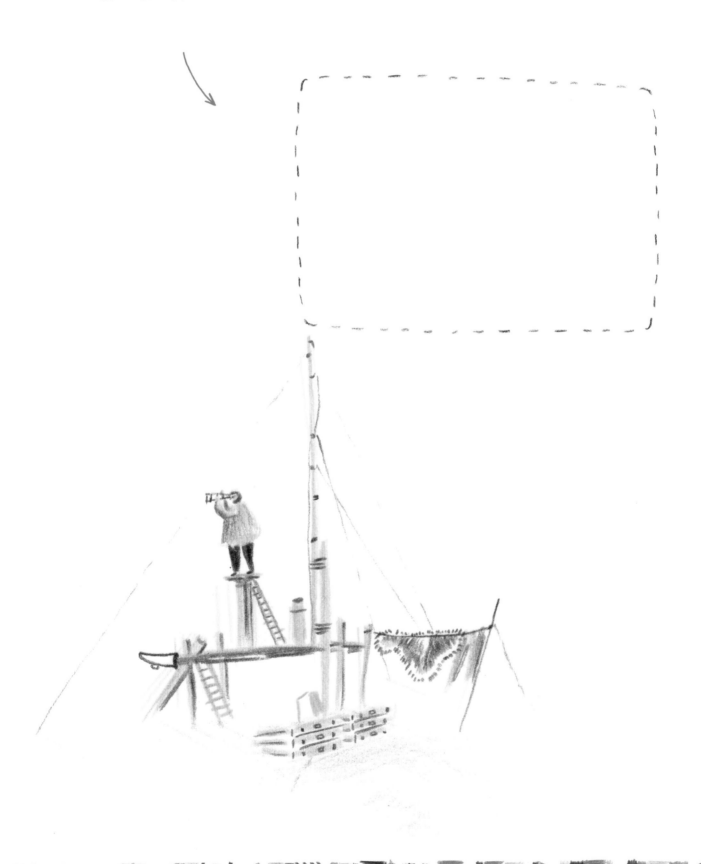

LABEL THE SHIP

BY MATCHING THE NUMBERED PARTS WITH THE WORDS AROUND THE ILLUSTRATION.

Bow

Norwegian Flag

Mast

Sail

Hull

Stern

Jib boom

Life Boats

3.

4.

2.

Keel

Answers at the back!

MAKE A PAPER BOAT

You WILL NEED

A rectangular sheet of paper or cardboard
Sticky tape

1. Lay the piece of paper on a flat surface. If the sheet is printed on one side, put the design you would like to appear on the outside of the boat facing up.

2. Fold in half from top to bottom, making a neat crease in the middle.

3. Fold the two corners of the folded edge inwards to meet in the middle, so that the top makes a point.

4. Now fold the loose rectangular ends of the paper up along the bottom of the triangles. Repeat on the other side.

5. You now have a hat. (Or a very simple boat).

6. Fold the bottom corners inward. Flip the boat over and fold the other side. Pull out the middle and push both points together to make a square.

7. Fold up the bottom flaps to the top point.

8. After you have folded both sides, pull out the middle to form a square.

9. Take the upper corners and pull them gently apart to create your paper boat.

10. Decorate as you like, adding tape to the bottom to make your vessel waterproof.

TIP
To make a simple boat, stop at step 5, then gently pull apart the sides of your boat from the bottom. Add tape to waterproof. It is now ready to sail!

1.

2.

3.

4.

5.

6.

7.

8.

9.

10.

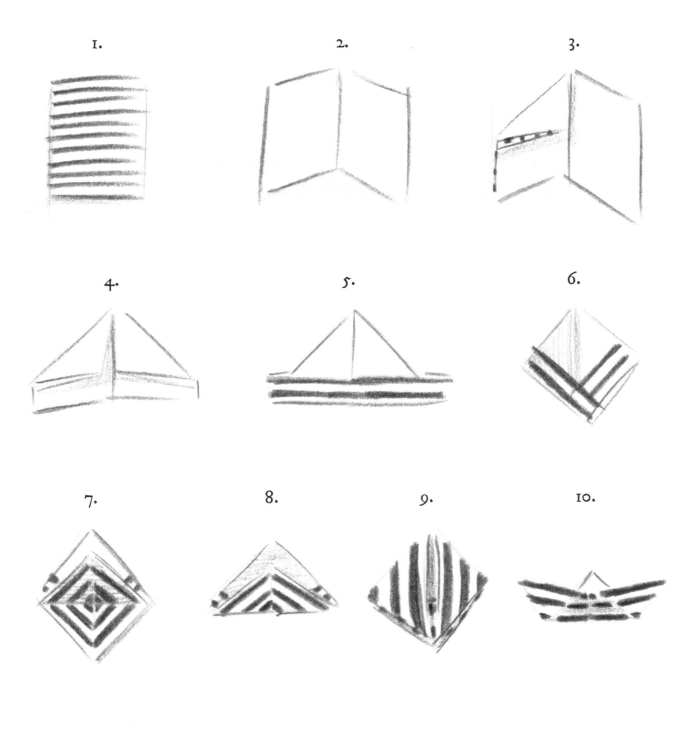

AND FINALLY ...

Find a stream (or a large bath tub) and race
your boat against a friend's.

DESCRIBE OR DRAW A DREAM YOU'VE HAD THAT YOU'D LIKE TO COME TRUE

FACT

Frank Worsley dreamt one night that Burlington Street in London was full of ice blocks and he was navigating a ship along it. When he went to the street the next morning, he saw the sign for Shackleton's Trans-Antarctic expedition and promptly signed up as ship's captain.

FACT

By the end of his journey, Shackleton hadn't washed for three months and hadn't changed his clothing for nearly a year!

DESIGN AN OUTFIT

TO KEEP YOU COMFORTABLE, WARM AND DRY IN THE ANTARCTIC.

TIPS

• Keep skin away from the elements to prevent frostbite. On Elephant Island, stowaway Percy Blackborrow had all the toes on his left foot cut off, because they were frostbitten and turning gangrenous.

• Try on items of clothing in your own wardrobe to find out which is warmest. Multiple layers will trap warm air close to the body.

• Choose between lightweight modern fabrics, tight woolen knits (like Shackleton) or animal skins. Roald Amundsen loved his sealskin suits!

• Don't go blind from looking at the snow. Protective eyewear is a must, as is a hat of some kind – the head can lose up to 20% of the body's heat.

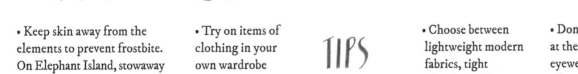

PACK FOR THE POLE

Shackleton packed plenty of equipment and supplies to keep everyone alive in Antarctica, from sledges and skis to blankets and mitts. Luckily, you've found some extra space in your cabin. **Which additional five items would you take with you?**

1

2

TIP

Your choice can be practical or sentimental.

3

4

5

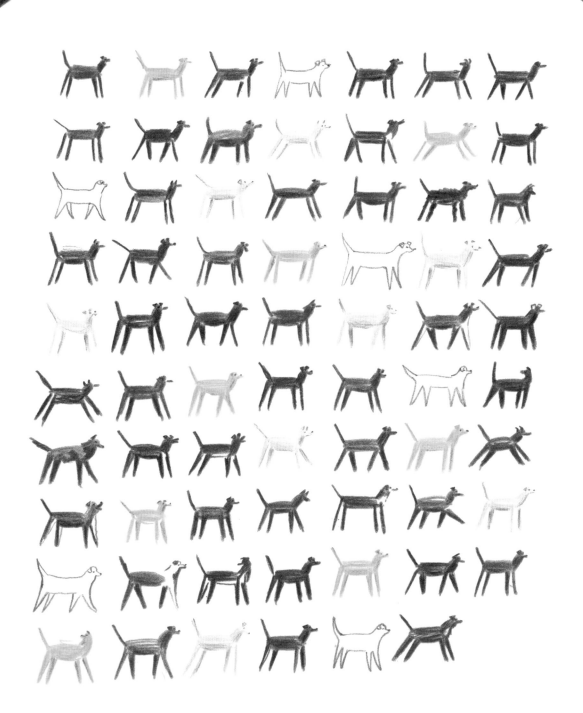

FACT

A much-loved cat, Mrs Chippy, came on board with the ship's carpenter Henry McNeish.
One month into the trip, they discovered that 'she' was in fact a male tabby, but by then
the name had stuck.

ADOPT A DOG

There were 69 dogs on board the Endurance. Since there was no professional dog trainer on the expedition, each one was assigned to a member of the team, and each was lovingly (if strangely) named. LOOK AT THE PICTURE OPPOSITE AND CHOOSE ONE DOG TO CARE FOR AND TRAIN.

MY DOG LOOKS LIKE THIS

Their name is ....

....

Their special trick is ....

....

ARCTIC OR ANTARCTIC?

They are both cold, dark places at the ends of the earth, but the Arctic (North Pole) and the Antarctic (South Pole) are polar opposites in more ways than one. How well will you fare in our polar challenge?

Questions

1. True or False: The Arctic is an icy land surrounded by ocean.
2. Where is the largest desert in the world?
3. Which pole is colder?
4. What is the largest land animal in Antarctica?
5. Why don't polar bears eat penguins?
6. What polar creature is nicknamed "the unicorn of the sea"?
7. Where are you most likely to find igloos?
8. The word "Arctic" comes from the Greek word Arktikos, which means "near the bear". Can you guess why it was given this name?
9. Did dinosaurs live in the Arctic or the Antarctic?
10. How long does a polar "day" last, from sunrise to sunset?

Answers at the back!

FACT

While a kitchen freezer's temperature is around -23°C
and human skin starts to freeze at around -18°C, winter in
Antarctica can fall below -80°C. The lowest temperature
ever recorded in the South Pole was -94.7°C.

DRAW AN ICE GIANT

"Standing on the stirring ice," Shackleton wrote, "one can imagine it is disturbed by the breathing and tossing of a mighty giant below." DRAW WHAT HE MEANT HERE.

A CROSSWORD TO CONQUER

Across

3   A magnetic instrument showing north, used in navigation. (7)

5   A dome-shaped hut made from hard snow. (5)

9   The most southerly continent on Earth, covered in snow and ice. (10)

10   A very strong wind. (4)

11   A shelter for dogs. (6)

Down

1   A heavy snowstorm. (8)

2   A sheet of floating ice. (4)

4   The most southerly point on Earth. (two words: 5, 4)

6   Fixed daily amounts of food. (7)

7   When a boat is overturned in water. (7)

8   An injury caused by exposure to extreme cold. (9)

DOG TOWN

During long periods waiting for spring, the crew built fancy "dog igloos" with porches and domes out of ice and wood for each of the ship's dogs. DESIGN AN IGLOO FOR YOUR FAVOURITE PUP.

FACT

Knowing that boredom was their biggest foe,
Shackleton kept his men busy with jobs every day
and amused at night with a variety of games, story-telling,
silly haircuts and singing contests.

As the ship drifted with the ice, they even had a 'Worst
Singer Onboard' competition, which Shackleton
handily won.

PLAN A VARIETY SHOW

To entertain your friends. Dress up. Recite a poem. Or make up a silly song about someone you know (on Elephant Island, the crew took turns doing this every week!). COMPLETE THE GAPS IN THE PROGRAMME WITH YOUR FAVOURITE ACTS.

Tuesday, 29th February, 1916

THE CREW OF ENDURANCE
present

ALL STAR VARIETY

⊕

1. Leonard Hussey & Banjo - It's a long way to Tipperary
2. ....
3. Dr. James McIlroy - Imitating the bagpipes

~ INTERVAL ~

4. Ernest Shackleton - Reading poems by Robert Browning
5. ....
6. ....

ARTISTIC DIRECTOR ....

THE GREAT ICE CUBE CHALLENGE

Shackleton recruited a scientific staff of four – a geologist, a biologist, a meterologist and a physicist – for his "great scientific expedition". Do you think any of them could pick up an ice cube with a piece of string, without tying any knots? IMPRESS FRIENDS AND CREW MATES WITH THIS SIMPLE TRICK.

You WILL NEED

A glass

1 large ice cube

A piece of string, about 20 cm long.

Table salt

1. Fill the glass to the top with water. Place the ice cube in the water. It will float.

2. Try to 'fish' for an ice cube with the string. It's impossible to 'catch' anything, right?

3. Now, lay the string across the ice cube and glass.

4. Sprinkle a layer of table salt over the ice and string. Leave for one minute.

5. Carefully pick up the ends of the string.

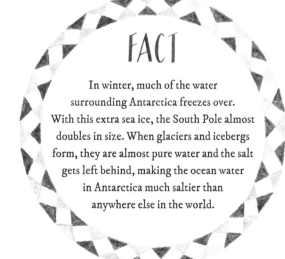

FACT

In winter, much of the water surrounding Antarctica freezes over. With this extra sea ice, the South Pole almost doubles in size. When glaciers and icebergs form, they are almost pure water and the salt gets left behind, making the ocean water in Antarctica much saltier than anywhere else in the world.

Record your findings here

....

....

....

....

....

....

....

....

....

....

....

What's happening?

Salt lowers the melting point of the ice. However, when salt is used in such a thin layer, like in this experiment, the water around the ice swiftly freezes again. The string gets trapped as the water around it refreezes, making it stick to the ice (though probably not so tightly as Endurance got stuck in the sea ice).

"[In No. 5 tent] there are eight of us living like sardines ... Clark sniffs the whole day long ... Lees and Worsley do nothing but argue and chatter about trivial matters, and the rest of us can do nothing to escape from it. Lees at night snores abominably ... At times like this ... my only relief is to take up my diary and write."

– Dr. Alexander Macklin,
Expedition surgeon

DEAR DIARY

Each member of the Endurance was encouraged to keep a journal to record their story of "high adventure, strenuous days [and] lonely nights." Imagine yourself in Shackleton's frozen camp at the bottom of the earth. WRITE A DIARY ENTRY, DOCUMENTING HOW YOU FEEL.

What can you see, hear, smell, touch and taste?

Are you missing home?

What are your thoughts on Shackleton and your chances of survival?

FACT

The Southern Lights are caused by giant explosions on the
surface of the Sun, which send fast-moving, electrically charged
particles streaming towards Earth. These are driven towards
the poles by the Earth's magnetic field – their varying
colours are a result of the different gases in the
upper atmosphere.

SOUTHERN LIGHTS

The tension of the polar nights was sometimes broken by the Southern Lights – a natural display of pink, purple, red and green hues swirling and twisting across the Antarctic sky. **FINISH THIS PICTURE BY SHOWING THE DRAMATIC LIGHTSHOW ABOVE THE CAMP.**

Use bright, fluorescent colours if you have them!

"Two sperm and two large blue whales were sighted,
the first we had seen for 260 miles. We also saw
petrels, numerous adélie, emperors, crab-eaters
and sea-leopards."

–Ernest Shackleton

DRAW THE ANIMALS THAT LIVE IN THE ANTARCTIC WATERS

FACT

Penguin poo – called guano – can be pink or orange as they mainly eat krill (which is pink).
The birds get together in such gigantic flocks, the mess they make on the
white snow can be spotted from space!

RECORD YOUR EVERYDAY ADVENTURES

Borrow a camera and take a series of shots that tell a dramatic story about your day.
Or alternatively, sketch the same thing. Edit your selection – you can only keep three pictures.

WHICH ARE THE BEST ONES TO SAVE AND WHY?

....

....

....

FACT

The expedition photographer Frank Hurley was "a warrior with his camera and would go anywhere or do anything to get a picture." He dove into icy water to retrieve his glass plate negatives after the Endurance sank, but he couldn't take all his photographs with him as the glass made them too heavy to carry. He had to pick out the best ones and smash the rest.

"Certainly a good deal of cheerfulness is due to the order and routine which Sir E. establishes wherever he settles down ... The regular daily task and matter-of-fact groove into which everything settles inspires confidence."

–Frank Worsley, Ship's captain

CAMP RULES

After the shipwreck, Shackleton knew that if his men sat about doing nothing they would become depressed, so he kept them busy with various jobs, giving each crew member a purpose and responsibility. Today you are in charge of Patience Camp. FILL IN THE SCHEDULE BELOW. ASSIGN JOBS AND FUN ACTIVITIES TO CREW MEMBERS AS YOU SEE FIT.

TODAY'S URGENT TASKS

1 ....

2 ....

3 ....

PLAN OF ACTION

MORNING ....

AFTERNOON ....

EVENING ....

To Do List

....

....

....

....

....

....

....

TIP

Daily activities at camp included: hunting for penguins and seals; cooking; eating; making tea; writing diary entries; tidying tents; washing and drying clothes; repairing kit; forecasting the weather; reading the Encyclopaedia Britannica and testing each other on it; enjoying a singalong.

FACT

In a turn of good fortune, the sea leopard was shot
and found to have a stomach full of undigested
fish, which provided a delicious meal for
the crew.

SEA LEOPARD ATTACK

One day, a ferocious sea leopard attacked Thomas Orde-Lees on the ice. Fortunately Frank Wild was quick on the scene with his trusty rifle. DRAW WHAT HAPPENED NEXT.

ESCAPING THE ICE

After six months on the ice, Shackleton and his men made a desperate dash to Elephant Island in three lifeboats. Match the captions below to the correct panels, then fill in the speech bubbles to show what Shackleton and his crew have to say on this treacherous journey.

A.

At night, the men camp on ice floes. When the ice splits, one of the men falls into the dark water.

B.

Despite the bitter days and nights, second-in-command Frank Wild remains cheery as ever, steering the boat on towards the warm prospect of breakfast.

C.

Luckily, Shackleton was nearby to rescue him. The Boss asks the drenched sailor if he is alright.

D.

Shackleton sees the ice beginning to break up and tells his crew it's time to move.

E.

Sailing is dangerous as fast, foamy water hurls blocks of ice to and fro, and killer whales threaten to capsize them.

F.

The 28 men get into three lifeboats. Their lives depend on them reaching land now.

PENGUIN FOR BREAKFAST

Imagine you are chef for the night on Elephant Island. Cook up a meal out of penguin, seal blubber, seaweed, limpets, dried milk and soggy biscuits and draw it here. On the second plate, add some luxuries from your own kitchen to lift morale.

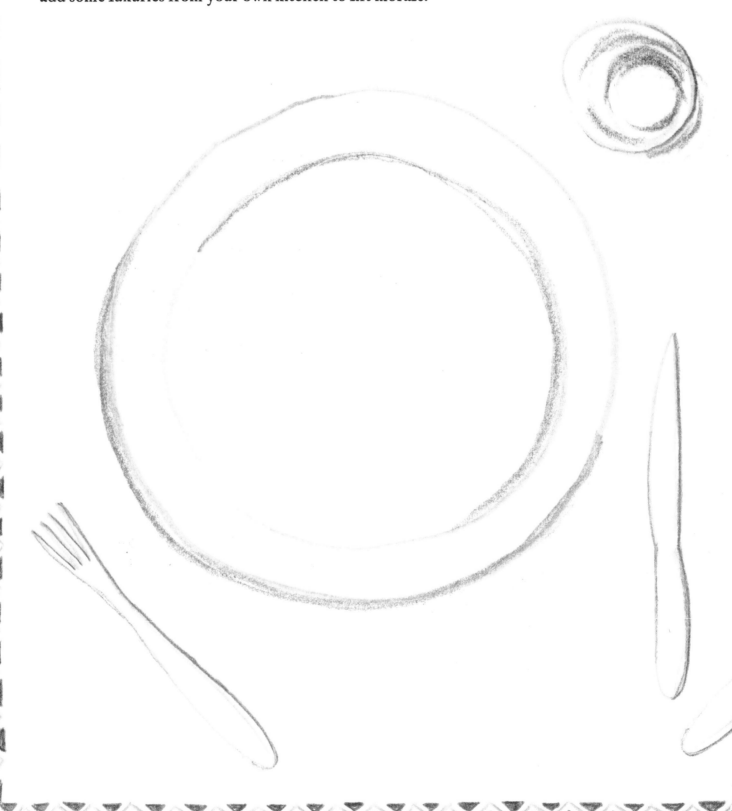

FACT

Each night in the Snuggery, the men would pore over a small penny cookbook they had carried to Elephant Island, dreaming about the treats they would eat when they got home. "We want to be fed ... like Korean babies," wrote one man, in his diary: "grossly overfed on nothing but porridge and sugar, black currant and apple pudding and cream, cake, milk, eggs, jam, honey and bread and butter till we burst, and we'll shoot the man who offers us meat."

IMAGINE BEING IN THE OPEN SEA

500 MILES FROM THE NEAREST CIVILISATION, ON A TINY BOAT.
FINISH THE ILLUSTRATION BY DRAWING WHAT YOU MIGHT
SEE ON THE JOURNEY.

'I called to the other men that the sky was clearing,
and then a moment later I realised that what I'd seen was not
a rift in the clouds but the white crest of an enormous wave.'

– Ernest Shackleton

MAKE A COMPASS

By magnetising a needle, you can make your own working compass, just like the one Frank Worsley used to navigate his way to South Georgia Island through the most treacherous seas in the world.

You WILL NEED

Cork or plastic bottle cap

Sharp knife or scissors

Needle

Bar magnet

Sticky tape

Shallow bowl of water

1. Cut a circle about one cm thick from the end of the cork, with scissors or a knife, and set to one side. Alternatively, you can use an upturned plastic bottle cap.

2. Magnetise the needle by stroking it with one end of the bar magnet 50 times from tail to tip. Stroke in one direction only – not back and forth – and lift the magnet away from the needle after each stroke to reduce the chance of de-magnetising.

3. Stick the needle to the cork or upturned bottle cap with some sticky tape and place it on top of the water. Position it in the centre of the bowl, well away from the edges.

4. The needle will slowly turn and eventually point from North to South. You can check the accuracy of this result by using a compass app on your smart phone, or a field compass, if you have one.

Be careful when using knives or scissors and handling sharp needles.

FACT

The Geographic South Pole should not be confused with the South Magnetic Pole (the one a compass actually points at), which is over 1,000 miles away.

Animals such as birds and whales use the Earth's magnetic field to find the right direction when migrating.

EXPEDITION MAP

This map needs labelling! Can you match the numbers on the map to the list below, to complete Shackleton's record of his expedition?

2.

6.

7.

5.

10.

8.

ATLANTIC OCEAN ....

INDIAN OCEAN ....

PACIFIC OCEAN ....

ANTARCTICA ....

THE SOUTH POLE ....

SOUTH GEORGIA ....

SOUTH AMERICA ....

ENDURANCE TRAPPED
IN HEAVY PACK ICE ....

ENDURANCE LOST ....

LIFEBOATS SET SAIL ....

9.

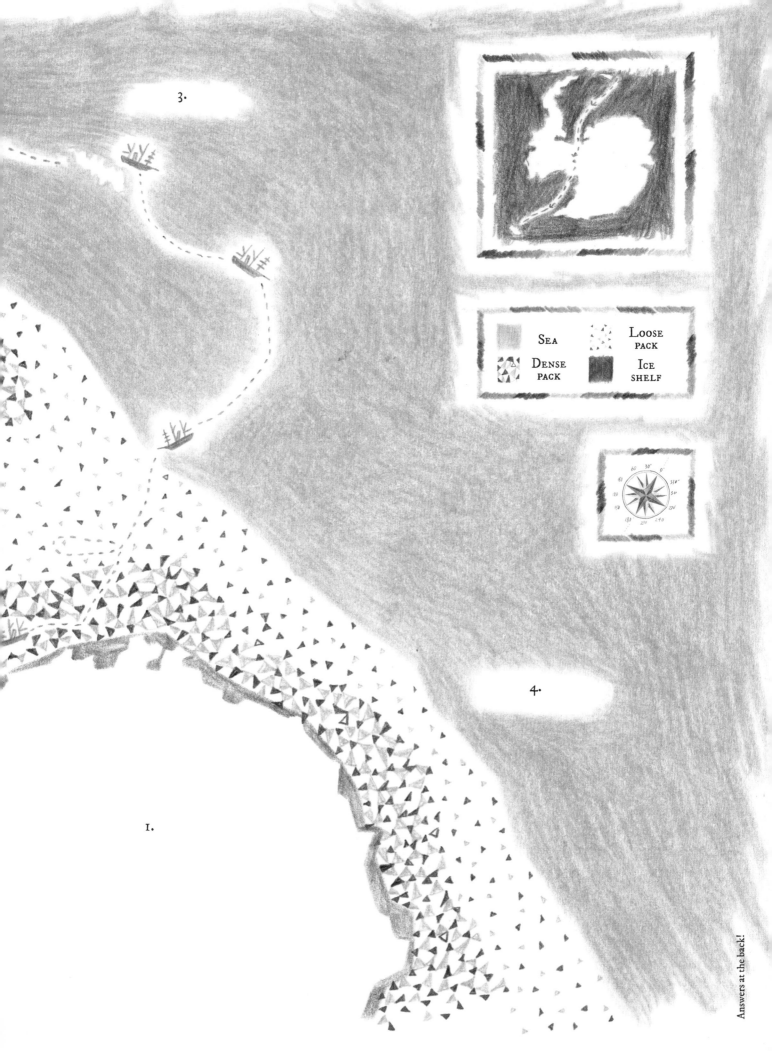

3.

SEA LOOSE PACK
DENSE PACK ICE SHELF

4.

1.

MAKE A DEN

To survive the violent weather on Elephant Island, the crew turned two of the lifeboats they had arrived in upside down and converted them into a shelter called the Snuggery. DRAW THE MEN'S NEW DEN HERE. Add a chimney, windows and anything else they may need.

PACK A SURVIVAL KIT

Imagine Shackleton has asked you to join him, Crean and Worsley to cross the unmapped mountains, gullies and glaciers of South Georgia to reach help. Put together a survival kit from things you have at home.

WHAT ITEMS ARE YOU TAKING WITH YOU AND WHY?

JOKE

Question: What do you call
a happy penguin?

Answer: A pen-grin!

GAME OF ENDURANCE

Can you survive shipwreck at the bottom of the Earth to battle impossible odds and make it out of Antarctica alive?

You will need

Two or more players

A dice

A character (see back flap)

Courage, luck & unwavering determination

How to Play the Game

Choose a crew member or Shackleton himself and place him on START. Throw your dice and follow the perilous route through pack ice, shipwreck, boredom, frostbite and the most treacherous seas in the world to complete your mission.

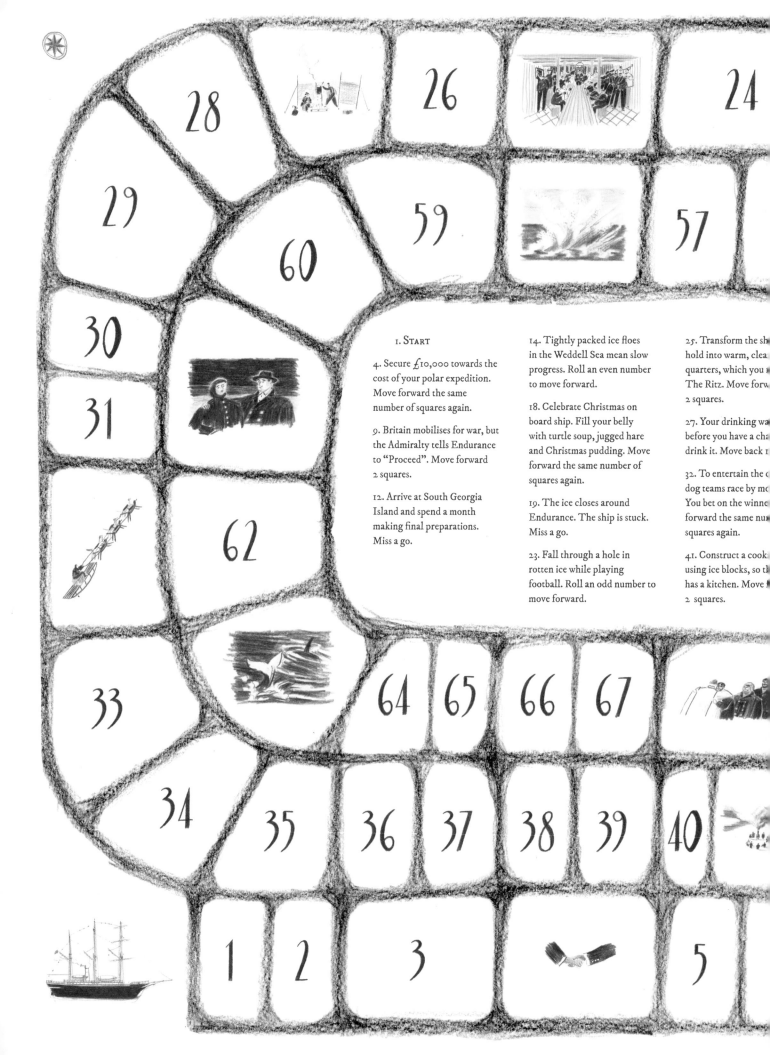

28

26

24

29

59

57

60

30

31

62

33

64 65 66 67

34

35 36 37 38 39 40

1 2 3 5

1. START

4. Secure £10,000 towards the cost of your polar expedition. Move forward the same number of squares again.

9. Britain mobilises for war, but the Admiralty tells Endurance to "Proceed". Move forward 2 squares.

12. Arrive at South Georgia Island and spend a month making final preparations. Miss a go.

14. Tightly packed ice floes in the Weddell Sea mean slow progress. Roll an even number to move forward.

18. Celebrate Christmas on board ship. Fill your belly with turtle soup, jugged hare and Christmas pudding. Move forward the same number of squares again.

19. The ice closes around Endurance. The ship is stuck. Miss a go.

23. Fall through a hole in rotten ice while playing football. Roll an odd number to move forward.

25. Transform the sh[ip's] hold into warm, clea[n] quarters, which you [call] The Ritz. Move forw[ard] 2 squares.

27. Your drinking wa[ter] before you have a cha[nce to] drink it. Move back [...]

32. To entertain the [...] dog teams race by mo[...] You bet on the winne[r...] forward the same nu[mber of] squares again.

41. Construct a cook[...] using ice blocks, so th[at...] has a kitchen. Move [...] 2 squares.

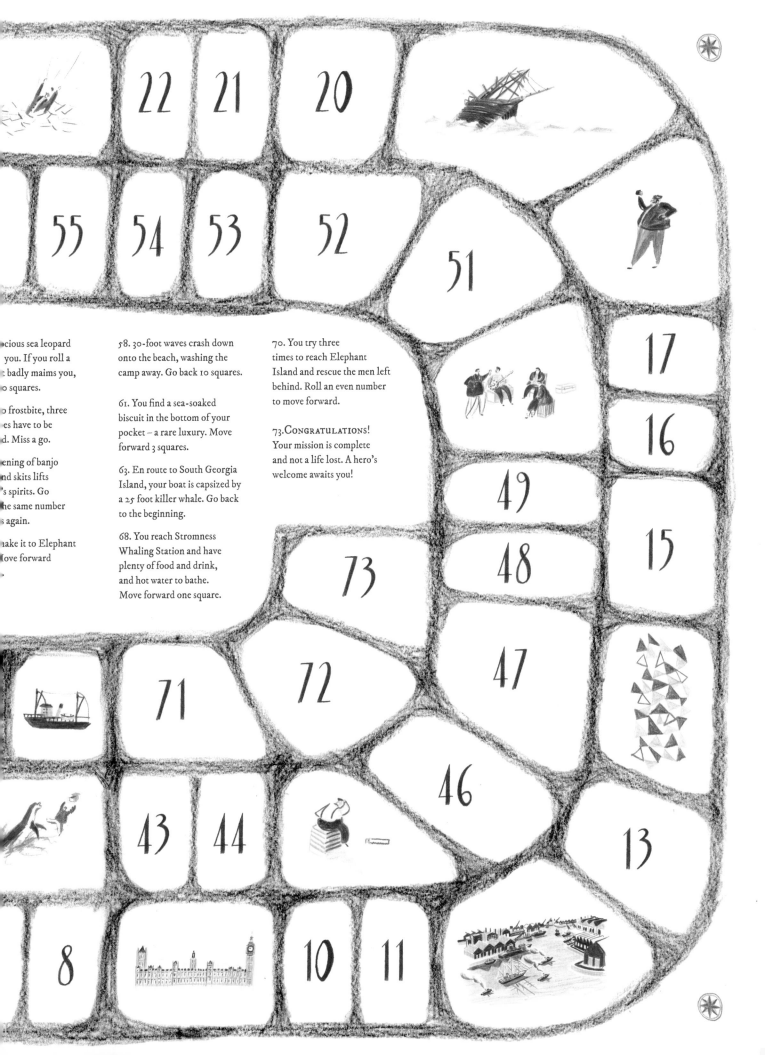

22 **21** **20**

55 **54** **53** **52** **51**

...cious sea leopard
... you. If you roll a
... badly maims you,
... squares.

... frostbite, three
...es have to be
...d. Miss a go.

...ening of banjo
...nd skits lifts
...'s spirits. Go
...he same number
... again.

...ake it to Elephant
...ove forward

58. 30-foot waves crash down
onto the beach, washing the
camp away. Go back 10 squares.

61. You find a sea-soaked
biscuit in the bottom of your
pocket – a rare luxury. Move
forward 3 squares.

63. En route to South Georgia
Island, your boat is capsized by
a 25 foot killer whale. Go back
to the beginning.

68. You reach Stromness
Whaling Station and have
plenty of food and drink,
and hot water to bathe.
Move forward one square.

70. You try three
times to reach Elephant
Island and rescue the men left
behind. Roll an even number
to move forward.

73. CONGRATULATIONS!
Your mission is complete
and not a life lost. A hero's
welcome awaits you!

17 **16** **15**

49 **48** **47**

73 **72** **46**

71 **13**

43 **44**

8 **10** **11**

"Life to me is the greatest of all games.
The danger lies in treating it as a trivial game ...
and a game in which the rules don't matter much.
The rules matter a great deal. The game has to
be played fairly, or it is no game at all. And even
to win the game is not the chief end. The chief
end is to win it honourably and splendidly."

–Ernest Shackleton

Solutions

Label the Ship

1. Keel, 2. Hull, 3. Bow, 4. Jib boom, 5. Mast,
6. Sail, 7. Stern, 8. Norweigan flag,
9. Life boats

Arctic or Antarctic?

1. False. The Arctic is an ice-covered ocean surrounded by land, while Antarctica is a continent covered with thick ice, surrounded by ocean.

2. Antarctica. Despite its thick ice, it is classed as a desert because so little moisture falls from the sky.

3. The South Pole. One reason is that Antarctica is the highest continent on Earth, and temperatures drop the higher you get.

4. A wingless midge that measures less than 1.3 cm long. There are no indigenous people on the continent. And penguins and seals don't live there either – they just visit.

5. Polar bears live in the Arctic and penguins are found in the southern hemisphere, so the chances of a polar bear catching a penguin the wild are zero!

6. The narwhal: a small whale with a long spiral tusk that lives in Arctic waters. Unscrupulous explorers used to pretend the beached narwhal tusks they found were magical unicorn horns. Queen Elizabeth paid £10,000 – the price of a castle – for one, and kept it with the crown jewels.

7. The North Pole. Despite the cold, approximately four million people live in the Arctic – including the Inuit people, who invented the igloo.

8. The name refers to two constellations that can be seen in the northern sky – Ursa Minor (the Little Bear) and Ursa Major (the Great Bear).

9. Both. A pygmy cousin of the T-Rex once lived in the Arctic. And 100 million years ago (before the deep freeze set in), numerous species of dinosaur flourished in Antarctica's lush rainforests.

10. A polar day lasts six months! Because of the earth's tilt and orbit around the sun, the poles experience only one sunrise and one sunset a year. For half the year, the sun never rises and it is dark, and for the other half the sun never sets and it is bright and sunny even at midnight!

A Crossword to Conquer

Across
3. Compass
5. Igloo
9. Antarctica
10. Gale
11. Kennel

Down
1. Blizzard
2. Floe
4. South Pole
6. Rations
7. Capsize
8. Frostbite

Escaping the ice

A - 4, B - 6, C - 5, D - 1, E - 3, F - 2

Expedition map

1. Antarctica
2. Atlantic Ocean
3. South Georgia
4. Indian Ocean
5. Pacific Ocean
6. South America
7. Lifeboats set sail
8. Endurance trapped in heavy pack ice
9. South Pole
10. Endurance lost